ANDREW JACKSON'S PRESIDENCY

PRESIDENTIAL POWERHOUSES

ANDREW JACKSON'S PRESIDENCY

CHRISTINE ZUCHORA-WALSKE

LERNER PUBLICATIONS ◆ MINNEAPOLIS

Lerner Publications Company
A division of Lerner Publishing Group, Inc.
241 First Avenue North
Minneapolis, MN 55401 USA

For reading levels and more information, look up this title at www.lernerbooks.com.

Main body text set in Caecilia LT Std 9.5/15.
Typeface provided by Adobe Systems.

Library of Congress Cataloging-in-Publication Data

Names: Zuchora-Walske, Christine.
Title: Andrew Jackson's presidency / by Christine Zuchora-Walske.
Description: Minneapolis, MN : Lerner Publications, 2015. | Series: Presidential powerhouses | Includes bibliographical references and index.
Identifiers: LCCN 2015000947| ISBN 9781467779265 (lb : alk. paper) | ISBN 9781467785488 (eb pdf)
Subjects: LCSH: Jackson, Andrew, 1767–1845—Juvenile literature. | United States—Politics and government—1829–1837—Juvenile literature. | Presidents—United States—Biography—Juvenile literature.
Classification: LCC E381 .Z83 2015 | DDC 973.5/6092—dc23
LC record available at http://lccn.loc.gov/2015000947

Manufactured in the United States of America
1-37517-18662-3/1/2016

★ TABLE OF CONTENTS ★

★ INTRODUCTION ★

It was March 4, 1837, and Andrew Jackson was no longer president of the United States. After eight years in office, he'd just handed over the presidency to his loyal vice president, Martin Van Buren. The festivities exhausted seventy-year-old Jackson, whose health was failing. He planned to stay at the White House for a few days afterward, gathering his strength for the journey home to Tennessee.

This wood engraving depicts President Martin Van Buren's inauguration in the US Senate chamber.

The White House in Jackson's time

The next day, while Jackson rested, a few friends stopped by to visit him. Among them were Missouri senator Thomas Hart Benton and Frank Blair, a newspaper publisher and a member of Jackson's informal circle of advisers. The men reminisced about Jackson's presidency. They talked about what Jackson had accomplished, and someone asked Jackson if he had any regrets.

"Only two," Jackson supposedly replied. "I regret I was unable to shoot Henry Clay or to hang John C. Calhoun."

Why would a president say such a thing about his colleagues in Congress? In modern times, if such a remark by the president were made public, it would likely bring instant condemnation.

But such a statement was not out of character for Jackson. He had built his career with tough actions and strong words. Like a lion, he could be both a stalwart protector and a ruthless predator.

It was no secret that Jackson disliked Clay and Calhoun. Clay had been a thorn in Jackson's side for two decades, criticizing Jackson's military leadership; stealing, in Jackson's view, the presidency from him in 1824; and opposing his economic policies. Jackson thought Clay, known as the Great Compromiser, was untrustworthy and opportunistic. As for Calhoun, Jackson found him haughty and cruel on a personal level and dangerously divisive on a political one. Jackson believed Calhoun's strident support for states' rights jeopardized the Union. And Jackson had, in fact, once threatened to hang Calhoun for it.

Jackson's strong language at the end of his presidency fit perfectly with his public persona. Jackson had been a wild youngster; a ferocious soldier; and a

John C. Calhoun

passionate, iron-willed, and heavy-handed political leader. He made it clear that in retirement, he would remain the same barely tamed American lion he'd always been.

Henry Clay

CHAPTER ONE

AN ADVENTUROUS LIFE

President Andrew Jackson was famous for his passionate style and strong-willed leadership. This personality was no act. It was a lifetime in the making. Jackson's colorful character got its start in a childhood brimming with both hardship and adventure.

A WILD CHILDHOOD

In 1765 Jackson's parents, Scotch Irish immigrants Andrew and Elizabeth Jackson, and their two young sons, Hugh and Robert, settled in the remote hill country of the British colonies. They lived in a log cabin on the border between modern North and South Carolina, in an area called the Waxhaw settlement. In early 1767, Elizabeth, who was pregnant, was left alone with her two boys when her husband died.

A few weeks later, on March 15, 1767, Andrew was born. Elizabeth Jackson moved her family to nearby Lancaster District, South Carolina, to live with her sister and serve as the housekeeper for her sister's large family. Andrew spent his first dozen or so years there.

The birthplace of Andrew Jackson, in the Waxhaw settlement near the border of North Carolina and South Carolina

Elizabeth Jackson wanted her youngest son to become a Presbyterian minister, so she took pains to provide him with an education, not a given in a region where there were few schools and teachers. Andrew attended an academy at the Waxhaw Presbyterian meetinghouse. There he learned to read, write, and "cast accounts," or do arithmetic. He also studied Greek, Latin, history, and the Christian Bible.

Andrew's academic performance was lackluster. He learned the Bible, and he picked up a knack for language that would eventually make him a good orator. But he never mastered Greek or Latin. His spelling skills were weak. And as Andrew grew, it became obvious to his community that he would never become a minister.

People expect a minister to set a good example. Andrew did the opposite. Elizabeth Jackson had her hands full managing the household, so she could not closely supervise her three sons and her sister's eight children. As a result, the children did largely as they pleased. Andrew developed a wild and mischievous character, and his stubborn streak and fiery temper went unrestrained. He was constantly playing pranks and cursing, even as a young boy. Andrew was fiercely loyal to anyone who agreed with him—but if anyone dared challenge him, he was more than willing to fight. Though he lost plenty of the fights he started, he always jumped right back up, ready to fight again.

THE AMERICAN REVOLUTION

Throughout Jackson's childhood, tensions were growing between Great Britain and its North American colonies. During this time, the British government banned settlements west of the Appalachian Mountains. The government wanted to avoid the cost of defending the settlers from American Indians, who resisted the colonists' encroachment on their land. This frustrated colonists, many of whom were eager to move away from the crowded eastern colonies and establish new homesteads. In addition, Britain taxed the colonies heavily and the colonists were not allowed to have representatives in the British Parliament. The government also tightly controlled trade in and out of the colonies, which caused financial hardships for the colonists.

In response to these and other problems, colonial leaders organized a Continental Congress in 1774 and again in 1775 to defend American colonists' interests and rights. The first fighting between British soldiers and colonial militiamen broke out in 1775. On July 4, 1776, the Continental Congress approved and published the United States' Declaration of Independence.

As the colonial rebellion transformed into a full-blown war, Jackson's childhood drew to a close.

Not all American colonists supported the American Revolution (1775–1783) and independence from Britain. In fact, nearly half were undecided or neutral, and 15 to 20 percent were Loyalists who supported British rule. Some 40 to 45 percent were patriots who believed that Americans would be much better off under self-rule. Loyalist sentiments were stronger in the Carolinas than in most of the other colonies, because the wealthy plantation owners there had strong family, financial, and emotional ties to Great Britain. But even in the Carolinas, patriots were fairly well represented.

The Jacksons were among the Carolina patriots. In 1779 Andrew's brother Hugh joined the patriot soldiers and soon died in battle. One year later, Andrew and his brother Robert joined too. In 1781 enemy soldiers captured them, and a British officer struck Andrew, causing severe injuries. The brothers were dragged off to prison, where they weakened under poor conditions and smallpox. Elizabeth Jackson managed to get them home, but Robert died within days. Andrew survived, only to lose his mother a few

While serving in the patriot army, Jackson (right) was captured by British soldiers and received a sword cut when he refused to clean an enemy officer's boots.

months later. She died of cholera while nursing her nephews on a British prison ship. At the age of fourteen, Andrew Jackson was an orphan. "I felt utterly alone," he later recalled.

Jackson's childhood experiences taught him several important lessons. He learned that he could survive tragedy, poverty, and hardship. He learned about the difficulty—and also the importance—of sacrifice in the cause of freedom. And he developed a heavy grudge against the British. He would never forget the misery his family, his community, and his country had suffered at British hands.

TENNESSEE LAWYER

For the next few years in the newly established United States, Jackson behaved like a wild teenager. He drank and gambled. He partied, danced, and played practical jokes. He called no single place home, instead bouncing from one relative or friend to another. Intermittently he held paying jobs, such as one at a saddler's shop. He did manage to finish school during this time and even worked as a country schoolteacher.

At the age of seventeen, Jackson decided that a proper career was in order. For a young man with no immediate family or fortune—but plenty of intelligence, ambition, and speaking ability—a law career was a good way to achieve a higher social and financial standing.

From 1784 to 1787, Jackson studied law as an apprentice to Spruce Macay, a lawyer in Salisbury, North Carolina. After earning his law license, Jackson accepted a job as a public prosecutor in the western district of North Carolina (modern-day Tennessee).

Jackson was touchy about his honor, and in 1788, he participated in his first duel. Dueling—formal, face-to-face battles between two combatants—had become a customary way for

men to defend their honor if they felt insulted. Rules governed these fights, and an apology to the offended party could stop a duel. Jackson wrote to a fellow lawyer who had insulted him in court, challenging the lawyer to a duel. "When amans feelings & charactor are injured the ought to Seek aspeedy redress," Jackson wrote, badly misspelling words as he was often known to do. "My charector you have Injured; and further you have Insulted me in the presence of a court and a larg audianc." Both men fired a shot, but neither was hit.

Throughout 1788 Jackson, several other attorneys, and a group of settlers traveled slowly west toward the small frontier town of Nashville. Along the way, Jackson bought his first enslaved African American, a woman named Nancy. Jackson wanted to climb the social ladder, and for white men, owning a slave was a status symbol—a display of money and power.

Almost immediately upon arriving in Nashville, Jackson met a young woman named Rachel Donelson Robards. She was the daughter of Nashville settlers John and Rachel Donelson and the wife of Lewis Robards. The Robards lived with Rachel's widowed mother when Jackson rented a cabin on Donelson's property.

Rachel Donelson Robards

Lewis Robards was a jealous man. Unfaithful himself, he suspected his wife of being unfaithful with every male acquaintance she made, including Jackson. After several months of Robards's angry accusations and threats, Jackson got fed up and found lodging elsewhere. This didn't calm Robards's jealousy, though, and he finally left his wife, moving north to Kentucky.

Sometime in 1789, Rachel and Andrew heard that Lewis Robards had begun divorce proceedings. In love by now, they eloped, traveling to Natchez, in Spanish territory (modern-day Mississippi) and returning in 1791 as husband and wife. In late 1793, they learned that the Robards's divorce had just been finalized. That made the Jacksons' marriage invalid, so they remarried officially on January 18, 1794.

Throughout the 1790s, Jackson worked hard with the goal of developing himself into a Tennessee gentleman. He earned enough money and fees paid in land to start a plantation of his own and to buy slaves to do the hard work of raising cotton on it. Jackson was appointed attorney general, to provide legal advice to the government of the Nashville area. The government also made him chief legal officer for the area's militia.

At this time, many newcomers to the area were living illegally on land belonging to American Indians, who launched frequent attacks to drive out the newcomers. During his frequent travels through the countryside, Jackson earned a reputation as a skilled evader of attacks by American Indians.

Jackson's political career began to develop. He was deeply involved in Tennessee's effort to become a state. He was also involved in naming the state. Feeling too many states had been named after individuals, he pushed for using the name of the river where the first settlements were. The word Tennessee comes from the Cherokee word Tanasi (of uncertain meaning) and was the name of an early Cherokee village along the banks of

the Little Tennessee River. When Tennessee became the sixteenth state in the Union in 1796, Jackson became its first member in the US House of Representatives. He followed this one-year job by serving as a US senator.

The jobs in Congress required living in Philadelphia, Pennsylvania, then the nation's capital. Living so far from home was expensive, and Jackson hated being away from Rachel, who stayed in Tennessee. In 1798 Jackson resigned his Senate seat so he could go home to his wife and find a more lucrative career.

This map shows the eastern part of the United States after Tennessee joined the Union in 1796. Jackson had been involved in efforts to make Tennessee a state.

In December 1798, he was elected as a judge to the Tennessee Superior Court. This job was prestigious, and it also paid well. He held it for six years and during this time also worked to stabilize his rocky finances. Through perseverance and great effort, he established a variety of general stores and businesses on his properties, some of which focused on boatbuilding, whiskey distilling, and horse breeding. He continued to practice law privately. In 1802 the Tennessee militia elected him its major general. In 1804 the Jacksons sold their house and farm and bought a farm they called the Hermitage, where they settled. Jackson quit his judgeship to focus on his personal and militia duties, recruiting and training men from all walks of life. He established more businesses nearby and continued to buy land and slaves.

The Jacksons moved to this log building on the Hermitage plantation in 1804.

BLOODY ANDREW JACKSON

Although Jackson worked hard to bolster his own financial, social, and political standing after settling in Tennessee, he remained a bit of a wild backwoodsman. He never outgrew his hot temper and his sensitivity to any perceived slight, and he kept getting into fights even after becoming a prominent citizen. In 1806 Jackson had a misunderstanding with Charles Dickinson, a fellow horse breeder. Jackson challenged the man to a pistol duel. Such fights were outlawed in Tennessee, so the men crossed the border to Kentucky. Dickinson fired first, hitting Jackson squarely in the chest. But Jackson didn't fall down. Instead, he aimed carefully, pulled the trigger, and killed his opponent. The bullet Dickinson fired at Jackson, however, lodged in Jackson's chest and stayed there, causing him pain for the rest of his life.

Andrew Jackson (left, with pistol) shot Charles Dickinson to death in a duel in 1806.

OLD HICKORY

In 1812 the United States declared war on Great Britain. Not fully accepting US independence, the British had refused to leave forts in the West and South and were arming American Indians for raids on US settlers. British naval officers on the high seas were capturing and impressing US sailors, or kidnapping them and forcing them into the British navy. These complaints and others led

Jackson (above), pictured in the uniform of a major general, US Army, offered his military services early on during the War of 1812.

to the War of 1812 (1812–1815). As soon as Jackson heard about the war, he offered his military services. President James Madison ordered Jackson to lead two thousand Tennessee militiamen to New Orleans, which had become part of the United States in the 1803 Louisiana Purchase.

Before they arrived, the War Department (the present-day Department of Defense) dismissed them without payment or supplies. Jackson had no choice but to carry out the devastating order to turn around. Earning the respect of his men, he personally paid for the supplies for the trip home. He gave up his horses so they could carry the sick and walked the entire 800 miles (1,287 kilometers) back—offering encouragement and gentle corrections and seeing to everyone's welfare the whole way. He wrote, "I led them into the field. I will at all hazard and risque lead them out."

During this trip, a soldier remarked that Jackson was tough as hickory, an extremely hard wood. Another affectionately called him Old Hickory, and the nickname stuck with him for the rest of his life.

Jackson gained further fame for his toughness and leadership throughout the War of 1812. In 1814 he delivered a resounding victory against the Creek, or Muskogee, Nation (in modern-day Alabama), whom he called a savage foe. He negotiated a treaty that forced the Creek out of the area. After this, the War Department named him a major general of the US Army. In late 1814, he led his troops to New Orleans to prepare for a British

After the Battle of Horseshoe Bend, Jackson (seated) negotiated a treaty with Creek leader William Weatherford, also known as Red Eagle (right), that forced the Creek out of the area.

invasion there. When that invasion came, Jackson's greatly outnumbered forces—much to everyone's surprise—crushed the British and forced them to leave Louisiana in January 1815.

The war had officially ended, but that news didn't reach the United States until a few weeks later. Jackson then took the helm of the US Army's Southern Division. He spent the rest of the decade in this role, focusing on what he saw as two key security problems along the southern border: the Spanish colony of Florida and the American Indians. He was ordered to subdue the Seminole Indians along the Florida-Georgia border. The Seminole had been raiding US settlements in the area, trying to drive out the white newcomers who had taken their land. Jackson interpreted his orders to mean he should invade Florida, which was the Seminole base of operations. He quickly captured two forts and ordered the arrest, trial, and hanging of two British citizens accused of helping the Seminole. Spain wasn't able to defend Florida against the United States, which claimed the region, so Spain signed a treaty ceding Florida to the United States. Meanwhile, Jackson used his tough reputation and threats of force to intimidate the leaders of the Cherokee, Chickasaw, Choctaw, and Creek nations of the southern United States into signing over large swaths of their land.

FROM HERO TO POLITICIAN

Jackson's performance in the War of 1812, as well as his land acquisitions from the Spanish and American Indians in following years, made him a hero in the eyes of like-minded Americans. In the 1820s, his career began to shift from military to political. In 1821 he served a short stint as Florida's first governor. In 1822 the Tennessee legislature nominated him as a candidate in the 1824 presidential election. Then, in 1823, the legislature elected him to the US Senate to build his political strength. (At the time,

This painting from 1910 depicts Jackson (in blue) at the Battle of New Orleans during the War of 1812. The war made Jackson a national hero.

senators were not elected by popular vote.) He used his Senate seat to convince the public that he was more than a fierce warrior and that he was neither a wild man nor a tyrant, as his opponents claimed. He kept his temper in check, made friends and political allies, and focused his work on military affairs—his field of expertise.

In 1824 Jackson ran for the presidency against four men who held federal posts: John Quincy Adams (secretary of state), William Crawford (secretary of the treasury), John Calhoun (secretary of war), and Henry Clay (Speaker of the House of Representatives). Jackson's popularity earned him by far the most popular and electoral votes. But because none of the candidates won a majority of electoral votes, it fell to the House of Representatives to choose the president. Clay formed an alliance in the House to successfully elect John Quincy Adams. Jackson and his supporters called this a "corrupt bargain," in which elite insiders ignored the will of the people.

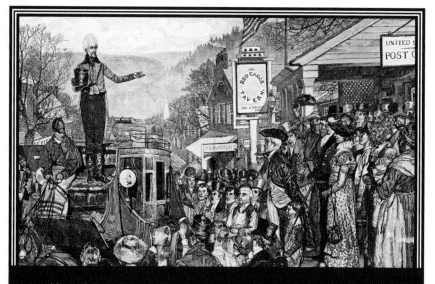

President-elect Jackson (left, standing) *delivers a speech from the driver's seat of his coach on his journey to Washington, DC, in 1828.*

Jackson and his supporters used this idea to campaign for the presidency in 1828. They established a new political party, which became known as the Democratic Party. It portrayed itself as the party of ordinary people and Adams's National Republican Party as the party of rich elites who used the government for their own benefit. President Adams's supporters painted Jackson as a bloodthirsty, greedy tyrant who stole another man's wife. They filled the newspapers with stories calling Rachel a bigamist—or someone who is illegally married to two people at once—since she had remarried before her divorce was legal.

But once again, Jackson's popularity prevailed. It carried him easily through all the mudslinging and into the presidency.

A SHAMEFUL CAMPAIGN

The 1828 presidential campaign took a heavy toll on Rachel Jackson. A gentle, kind, and pious person, she found the accusations about her marriage and her husband extremely stressful. In addition, she dreaded assuming the role of First Lady, feeling she lacked the poise and confidence of First Ladies who'd come before her. When she heard of Jackson's victory, she said, "For Mr. Jackson's sake, I am glad; for my part, I never wished it." Her health had deteriorated during the long campaign, and on December 22, 1828, sixty-one-year-old Rachel Jackson died, probably of a heart attack. She would never reside in the newly built White House, and Andrew Jackson would grieve her loss for the rest of his life.

He blamed his foes for her death, saying they had "[abused] that blessed one who is now safe from suffering and sorrow, whom they tried to put to shame for my sake."

Rachel Jackson (above) suffered from poor health over the course of the long and stressful presidential campaign.

★ CHAPTER TWO ★

SHAKING
UP THE
ESTABLISHMENT

When Jackson began his presidency, the government had been under the control of a relatively closed group of people. This had been true since the country's founding. All the nation's first six presidents had been either wealthy landowners in Virginia or members of influential families in Massachusetts. And all had used their influence to secure high government positions for members of their elite circle. John Quincy Adams was even the son of the second president, John Adams. In comparison, Jackson was a complete outsider. Under this new president from outside the elite, the balance of power in the federal government would shift dramatically. He had little to lose by shaking up the system, and that's exactly what he did.

THE SPOILS SYSTEM
One of Jackson's first accomplishments as president was to reform the federal government bureaucracy. Before Jackson, government officials could generally count on keeping their jobs for their lifetime. But the new president believed that this

John Marshall (right), chief justice of the Supreme Court, swears in Jackson (left) at the US Capitol during his first presidential inauguration on March 4, 1829.

practice made people lazy, entitled, corrupt, and dictatorial. He explained, "They are apt to acquire a habit of looking with indifference upon the public interests and of tolerating conduct from which an unpracticed man would revolt. Office is considered as a species of property." What is more, Jackson believed that any intelligent man could carry out the duties of such government offices, so extensive experience in office really wasn't necessary—and it certainly wasn't worth the corruption it fostered.

Jackson's campaign had accused the Adams administration of using the US government for its own private gain. The American people had agreed with Jackson and subsequently not reelected Adams to a second term. Jackson finished the job by removing those he saw as Adams's minions.

JACKSON'S INAUGURATION

Legend says that Andrew Jackson's inauguration party was a raucous mob scene. According to some stories, after Jackson was sworn in on March 4, 1829, hundreds of ill-behaved guests followed him into the White House, drank heavily to celebrate his victory, and created chaos. This story was easy to believe for anyone who'd been paying attention to the presidential campaign. Jackson's opponents had painted him as a violent, uncouth, and wild man.

But modern historians who have studied eyewitness accounts say the legend is an exaggeration. It was customary for the White House to open to the public so citizens could congratulate the new president in person. Because Jackson was so popular, the White House became crowded with well-wishers, and a noisy, packed, and at

times chaotic scene resulted. In fact, at one point, Jackson even got pinned to a wall by the enthusiastic guests and was rescued by his staff and brought to a hotel. Meanwhile, other staffers brought the whiskey-laced punch served at the party out to the lawn—and the partiers followed.

According to legend, Jackson's inauguration party was a wild affair.

Jackson started with members of his official cabinet of advisers. He installed a new secretary of state (Martin Van Buren), secretary of the treasury (Samuel Ingham), secretary of war (John Eaton), and secretary of the navy (John Branch). He also established an informal council of advisers made up of longtime colleagues, supporters, and friends. This council became known as Jackson's kitchen cabinet. He continued his bureaucratic reforms with replacements among land officers, customs officers, and federal marshals and attorneys. These replacements made up only about 10 to 20 percent of the positions over which Jackson had power, but the changes seemed drastic compared to the few made by his predecessors.

Jackson's intentions—at least those he stated publicly—were good, but the results of his housecleaning were mixed. He did get rid of some corrupt, drunken, or otherwise incompetent officials. But he made his removals hastily, sometimes simply because the official had supported Adams. In some cases, Jackson fired perfectly decent people for flimsy reasons, leaving many families in dire financial straits. Jackson's new appointments were not always ethical or wise. He claimed that honesty and efficiency were his goals, but when choosing replacements, he relied solely on his own friendships and the advice of his friends and supporters. He made many appointments as rewards for political favors. Several of these went to newspaper editors, which made people wonder whether freedom of the press would continue under President Jackson.

In Jackson's time, newspapers were the main way information spread across the nation. Newspapers were often politically biased, and when politicians bestowed favors on newspaper editors, it might tempt the editors to spin the news to make those politicians look better. Thomas Ritchie, a newspaper editor and Jackson supporter, recognized the risks in Jackson's

FREEDOM OF THE PRESS

The First Amendment to the US Constitution defines several of the most cherished rights of citizens, including freedom of the press. This amendment reads: "Congress shall make no law respecting an establishment of religion, or prohibiting the free exercise thereof; or abridging the freedom of speech, or of the press; or the right of the people peaceably to assemble, and to petition the Government for a redress of grievances."

The First Amendment guarantees Americans the right to express and access a wide variety of ideas. Among other things, it means that Americans can freely share facts, opinions, and ideas verbally and nonverbally—through books, newspapers, public meetings and demonstrations, art and, in modern times, the Internet, television, radio, photography, film, and more—without fear of punishment.

Two women and a man operate a printing press in this illustration from 1822.

appointments. In a letter to his secretary of state, Martin Van Buren, he advised against appointing editors: "Invade the freedom of the press . . . by showering patronage too much on editors of newspapers . . . and the rights of the people themselves are exposed to imminent danger." Jackson, for his part, scoffed at the idea that he would make any removals or appointments that weren't in the public's best interest.

Jackson called his new approach to government bureaucracy rotation in office. But it became known more commonly by another name: the spoils system. The governor of New York, William Marcy, defended Jackson's actions by pointing out that when politicians "are contending for victory, they avow their intention of enjoying the fruits of it. If they are defeated, they expect to retire from office. They see nothing wrong with the rule that to the victor belongs the spoils." From this time forward, all US presidents followed the spoils system.

War secretary John Eaton (above) set off a scandal when he married Peggy (O'Neal) Timberlake.

THE EATON AFFAIR

One of Jackson's new appointments triggered a different sort of Washington shakeup. This episode was essentially a social conflict. But because it occurred among the highest-ranking members of Jackson's administration, the conflict had a far-reaching political impact.

Jackson's war secretary, John Eaton, was the only member of the president's cabinet who was a close, longtime friend. They

were neighbors back in Tennessee. The two had served together in the army and US Senate, and Eaton had strongly supported both of Jackson's presidential bids. Jackson was especially glad to have Eaton aboard, because the rest of Jackson's official administration was made up of men he barely knew. Eaton's personal life, however, caused some problems among the other cabinet members. Shortly before accepting his new post, he had married Margaret (Peggy) O'Neal Timberlake, whose first

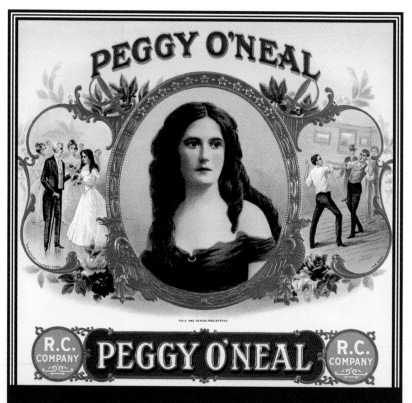

This cigar box label features Peggy O'Neal and two scenes from her life. President Jackson offers her flowers (left) after she was snubbed by the other wives of his cabinet members, and her husband kills another man in a duel for insulting her (right).

husband, naval officer John Timberlake, had recently died at sea. Rumor had it that John Timberlake had killed himself after learning that she was having an affair with John Eaton.

The cabinet members' wives considered the Eatons' marriage questionable, if not outright immoral. Rumors spread that she had also had lovers while working in her father's bar.

Women at the time lived with a double standard: they were supposed to remain virgins before marriage and sexually faithful afterward, while standards were not as strict for men. Respectable middle- and upper-class white women were not supposed to work outside the home or appear to take an interest in government. Smart and outgoing, Peggy Eaton had broken these rules by socializing with male politicians. The cabinet members' wives found her behavior socially unacceptable, and they refused to socialize with her. They pressured their husbands to socially shun the Eatons too.

The shunning of Peggy Eaton incensed Jackson. It reminded him of the horrible treatment his beloved Rachel had suffered. He suspected that someone in his administration—namely his vice president John Calhoun, whose wife Floride led the social boycott against the Eatons—was trying to isolate him from his only friend and gain control of his administration. Jackson jumped to the Eatons' defense. So did Van Buren, who was a widower and less involved in the elite Washington social scene than his colleagues were.

Before long, the Eaton Affair nearly paralyzed Jackson's administration. Social pressures and high emotions all around made it difficult for the men to work together effectively. Meanwhile, Jackson was becoming preoccupied with collecting evidence to defend the Eatons and to defame the Eatons' persecutors. To solve this dilemma, Van Buren offered to resign in 1831 and said Eaton should too. Jackson accepted this plan and

BIRDS OF A FEATHER

Gossip often surrounded public figures during Jackson's time, much as it does in the modern era. Margaret Bayard Smith was a Washington, DC, socialite and writer during the early years of the United States. In a letter written on January 1, 1829, she insulted both John Eaton's future wife and Jackson's wife, Rachel. (Smith was unaware that Rachel had just died.)

> Eaton . . . is to be married to a lady whose reputation [has been] has totally destroyed . . . She has never been admitted into good society, is very handsome and of not an inspiring character and violent temper. She is, it is said, irresistible and carries whatever point she sets her mind on. [Jackson's] personal and political friends are very much disturbed about it; his enemies laugh and divert themselves with the idea of what a suitable lady in waiting Mrs. Eaton will make to Mrs. Jackson and repeat the old adage, "birds of a feather will flock together."

Margaret Bayard Smith

then asked the other cabinet members to resign, which they did. Jackson appointed new cabinet members to replace them. The Eatons moved to Florida, where John became governor.

Eventually Calhoun became so estranged from Jackson, both socially and politically, that he too resigned, leaving the vice presidency vacant. Meanwhile, Van Buren's support had endeared him to Jackson, and he became the president's choice for vice president when Jackson ran for—and won—reelection in 1832.

★ CHAPTER THREE ★

THE AMERICAN SYSTEM AND ABOLITIONISM

Jackson's first term as president brought with it a great deal of upheaval in government personnel. But that was just one of several controversies simmering at the time. Another complex issue Jackson had to manage was an economic policy known as the American System (1816–1828).

THE AMERICAN SYSTEM

The American System had two key elements: a tariff on certain imported goods and federal funding for infrastructure projects such as roads and canals. This economic system was designed to help the young United States grow its economy and infrastructure, provide more for its people, and depend less on other nations.

The American System tariff placed a tax on manufactured goods imported from Europe. US manufacturers had sprung up in the years before and during the War of 1812, when the United States had outlawed trade with Great Britain (and for part of that time with France too). But these young businesses had difficulty competing with well-established European factories, which could produce goods much more cheaply. A tariff on imported cloth, clothing, iron, hemp, fur, flax, and liquor raised prices on those products and encouraged Americans to buy cheaper items from US manufacturers instead, which in turn encouraged those businesses to grow. More US manufacturing and less importation allowed the country to be less affected by events in Europe. A tariff on imports served a second goal as well. The money it brought in was a key source of revenue for the federal government.

Jackson during his first term in office

Some of this revenue was used to reduce the nation's debt to foreign nations, which had piled up during the war years. And some was used to fund infrastructure and transportation projects, which US senator Henry Clay, the American System's most enthusiastic congressional promoter, called internal improvements. The United States had two important reasons to improve its roads, canals, bridges, and other infrastructure. First, poor transportation infrastructure had been a big problem during the War of 1812. It had hampered the United States' ability to move troops, supplies, and information effectively. Second, infrastructure was key to developing the US economy. To move US agricultural products and manufactured goods to market around the country, the nation needed more and better travel routes.

Overall, the American System did achieve its goals. By the 1820s, American manufacturing had grown substantially. Transportation had also improved. However, the system had its drawbacks as well. It was designed to help integrate the various parts of the US economy, but in practice, it created quite a bit of internal conflict. Federal subsidies for infrastructure projects

The southern economy, which was mostly agricultural, was hit hard by tariffs. This image shows enslaved African Americans harvesting cotton, an important crop in the South in Jackson's time and beyond.

tempted contractors to bribe their congressional representatives for preferential treatment. Yet another, more serious, problem evolved over time. It became obvious that the system was benefiting the northern states more than the southern states. The North was becoming more industrial, while the South stayed mostly agricultural, using slave labor to produce cotton and other crops. Northern factories were shielded from competition with European ones, because tariffs raised the cost of imported products. Meanwhile, the southern economy took a double punch to the pocketbook. The South had few manufacturing facilities, so it had to buy products from northern manufacturers or European ones. Either way, those products were expensive. And the tariff shrank demand for European products, which meant that European manufacturers bought less cotton and other crops from the South, which depended on this source of income.

THE NULLIFICATION CRISIS

In 1828 Congress passed a higher-than-ever tariff. This infuriated white southerners, who called it the Tariff of Abominations. Calhoun prepared a forceful opposition to the tariff. (Calhoun was vice president under Adams at the time. He continued in that position under Jackson.) Later the same year, Calhoun wrote a document called the "South Carolina Exposition and Protest," which explained why he believed that the 1828 tariff was unconstitutional. It also claimed that each state had the right to nullify, or cancel, inside its borders any law it considered unconstitutional. A state could do this by assembling a nullification convention. If 75 percent of the other states agreed the law *was* constitutional, the dissenting state could secede from the Union, or leave the United States.

Southern opposition to the tariff, as well as all the other problems with the American System, fell to Jackson to deal

SHOWDOWN AT THE JEFFERSON DINNER

In the early nineteenth century, Washington politicians celebrated the April 13 birthday of third president Thomas Jefferson with a dinner. Calhoun and Jackson were both speakers. Calhoun and many of the other speakers collaborated to offer a series of toasts that they hoped would give nullification an official air and would suggest that Jefferson would have smiled upon it. Jackson got wind of the plan the night before and prepared a comeback. His turn came after several of the nullifiers' toasts. The crowded room went silent, and all eyes were on Jackson. Jackson stood, raised his glass, and growled succinctly, "Our Federal Union—it *must* be preserved." Calhoun took his turn next. He rambled, "The Union, next to our liberty the most dear. May we all remember that it can only be preserved by respecting the rights of the States, and distributing equally the benefit and burden of the Union." Calhoun got the last word, but his plan had backfired. Jackson had embarrassed Calhoun in public by disagreeing with him. Jackson had shown that as always, he could not be intimidated.

Thomas Jefferson

with once he became president in early 1829. As a senator, Jackson had supported the American System. He, like many of his colleagues, had seen it as a way to build the United States' economic power and independence and to aid in the nation's defense. But as president, he began to realize the system's problems. In particular, he found the scrambling for favors that he saw in Congress to be shameful. He worried that tariffs and infrastructure projects were encouraging corruption. And he loathed the regional squabbling brought on by the system. He thought the secessionist ideas of the nullifiers were especially dangerous. He believed that preserving the Union, which gave Americans strength in numbers, was the only way to preserve US liberty. He had acquired this belief through decades of struggle with the British, American Indians, and the Spanish.

So in 1830, Jackson began vetoing transportation bills, refusing to sign them into law. And in 1831, he urged Congress to reduce tariff rates. In July 1832, Congress lowered some rates but kept the high rates for cloth and iron. South Carolina responded by calling a nullification convention. In November this convention declared the tariffs of 1828 and 1832 unconstitutional and prohibited customs agents from collecting those taxes within South Carolina. A month later, Calhoun resigned as vice president to become a US senator of South Carolina, his home state.

Meanwhile, Jackson responded to the nullification crisis on two fronts. He wanted both to make peace with the nullifiers and to show them that he meant business. So he encouraged Congress to reduce tariff rates even further. He issued a Nullification Proclamation explaining to the public, in great detail, why the Union must be preserved and why South Carolina's actions were so dangerous. He ended with a dramatic appeal to his fellow citizens to heed the "crisis in our affairs, on which the continuance of our unexampled prosperity, our

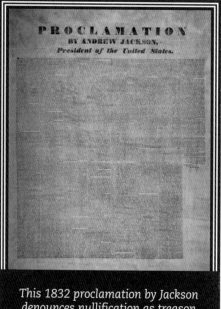

This 1832 proclamation by Jackson denounces nullification as treason and rebellion and warns South Carolinians to obey the laws.

political existence, and perhaps that of all free governments may depend."

Calhoun and Clay worked together in the Senate to negotiate the Compromise Tariff of 1833. This bill established an automatic series of tariff reductions to occur between 1833 and 1842. It was accompanied by a Force Bill, which authorized Jackson to use military force if necessary to collect customs duties on imported products. Both measures passed. Calhoun and eight fellow senators stalked out of the Senate chamber upon passage of the Force Bill, but much to everyone's relief, Jackson never found cause to use it. The crisis had passed.

THE ABOLITIONIST MOVEMENT

Calhoun vehemently opposed the American System not only because it caused financial hardship for southern plantation owners but also because he believed it put the South's economy—which depended on the labor of slaves—in grave danger. Calhoun didn't like the direction in which the US economy was headed. The importation of enslaved people, though not slavery itself, had been outlawed nationwide in 1808. The northern states were growing ever more industrial, and nine of them had already outlawed slavery within their borders. Even the southern slave

THE WHIGS

The Calhoun-Clay alliance of 1833 led to the formation of a new political party, the anti-Jackson Whig Party. The members of the Whig Party didn't agree with one another on the American System or on the movement to end slavery, but they shared a loathing for the way Jackson had dealt with issues. They accused Jackson of acting like a king—doing as he pleased despite the will of Congress. The Whig Party borrowed its name from a group of early American patriots who had opposed the British monarchy. Though not all Whig Party members opposed slavery, Webster and Clay both did. Clay owned slaves himself but worked for the gradual end of slavery and the colonization of freed African Americans in Africa. He also opposed the resettlement of the American Indians of the southeastern United States to lands west of the Mississippi.

Prominent Whig Party members Daniel Webster (left) and Henry Clay (right)

states that bordered northern ones, such as Maryland, were growing more industrial. As that happened, slavery grew less viable, the number of slaves dropped, and activists who wanted to abolish slavery gained power.

Calhoun believed that if the interests of northern industry continued to trump those of southern agriculture, the South's way of life, based on the belief that whites were superior to blacks, was doomed. Calhoun and his supporters fought the tariff both to protect the southern economy and to test the extent of federal power over states' rights.

Jackson understood exactly what Calhoun was up to. The president refused to give up any federal power over the southern states because he believed that doing so jeopardized the Union. He said, "The wickedness, madness, and folly of the leaders and the delusion of their followers . . . to destroy themselves and our Union has not its parallel in the history of the world. The Union will be preserved."

On the surface, this act may have appeared to be a stand against slavery. After all, some nullifiers claimed that the tariff was an abolitionist act. With it, they said, the North was trying to impose its antislavery values on the South. And Jackson himself claimed to be "the representative of the 'common man.'" But Jackson's priority was first and foremost to preserve the Union, not to oppose slavery.

During Jackson's administration, ordinary working-class people did gain rights they had never before enjoyed—especially the right to vote. (In the early United States, only landowners could vote.) But these rights stopped with white men. They didn't extend to women, American Indians, or African Americans.

Jackson was no abolitionist. He had grown up in South Carolina, where most white Americans perceived slavery as a normal part of life. When he grew up and moved to Tennessee,

he became a slave owner himself. Enslaved men, women, and children labored on his plantations and in his various business enterprises and waited on his family. Congress had outlawed the international slave trade in 1808, but slave trading in slaveholding states remained legal, and Jackson was also engaged in this trade, buying and selling African Americans throughout his presidency.

Meanwhile, the US antislavery movement had been gathering strength. Some activists believed white and black people could never integrate, and they wanted to send free African Americans to establish colonies in Africa. A group of white Americans created the American Colonization Society in 1816 to pursue this idea. They raised money to buy slaves' freedom and a piece of land in West Africa, where freed people moved. The settlement there became the nation of Liberia in 1824.

Other activists and most free northern African Americans opposed colonization. They wanted to abolish

Abolitionists commonly circulated publications such as this 1837 antislavery poem, "Our Countrymen in Chains," by John Greenleaf Whittier.

slavery immediately, without payment to slave owners, and see US society fully integrated. These abolitionists saw slavery in America as a moral outrage, a disease that would eventually damage or even destroy the nation. And they were outspoken and persistent. Its members sent petitions to state officials and to Congress. They ran for public office, campaigning on abolitionist principles. They published and distributed abolitionist literature.

Jackson viewed abolitionism the same way he viewed nullification: as a threat to the Union. He acted just as decisively to try to silence the abolitionists as he had to squash the concept of nullification. When the New York Anti-Slavery Society sent abolitionist literature to religious and civic leaders in the South in 1835, slavery supporters rioted in Charleston, South Carolina.

Jackson responded by forbidding the post office to deliver abolitionist literature in the South. And in 1836, in direct contradiction of the First Amendment's guarantee of free speech, Jackson's administration supported a gag rule, a resolution passed in the US House of Representatives to prohibit any discussion in Congress of topics related to slavery.

The gag rule horrified Jackson's old rival, John Quincy Adams, who had become a representative from Massachusetts. As described by Harriet

John C. Calhoun (above) *supported the gag rule.*

Martineau, a social scientist of the time, Adams "fought a stout and noble battle in Congress . . . in favour of discussion of the slavery question, and in defence of the right of petition upon it; on behalf of women as well as of men." Adams blasted the illegality of the gag rule, manipulating House procedures in order to bring up slavery over and over again. Thanks to Adams's years of persistence, the House finally ended the gag rule in December 1844.

John Quincy Adams (above) fought persistently to bring the gag rule to an end.

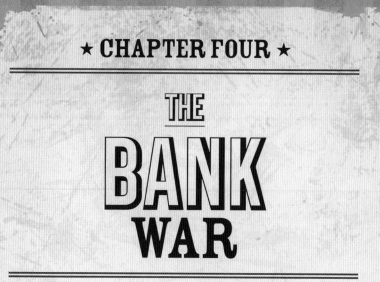

★ CHAPTER FOUR ★

THE BANK WAR

When Jackson's opponents in Congress accused him of acting like a king, they weren't just referring to his heavy-handed dealings with nullifiers and abolitionists. They were also referring to his actions toward the Bank of the United States.

THE FIRST BANK OF THE UNITED STATES

Congress had chartered (issued a legal document to establish) the Bank of the United States, known as the First Bank, in 1791. Its purpose was to help the nation deal with the aftermath of the American Revolution, which had left the federal government and the states with huge debts. Meanwhile, the paper money that the Continental Congress had issued to finance the war had become worthless. The US government established the First Bank in Philadelphia to stabilize the nation's financial system. The bank consolidated the federal and state debts. It attracted wealthy stockholders who had an interest in the nation's well-being. It collected taxes, served as a depository for federal funds, paid the US government's bills, made loans to the government, and

From the beginning of his presidency, Jackson opposed the Bank of the United States.

established a standard national currency. It also took deposits from and made loans to private citizens and businesses.

The charter of the First Bank of the United States expired in 1811. Instead of renewing the charter, Congress let it expire because many of the bank's original opponents, such as presidents Thomas Jefferson (1801–1809) and James Madison (1809–1817), still opposed it. Opponents believed that a national bank was unconstitutional. They worried that it would monopolize banking and make it impossible for other banks to survive.

Then came the War of 1812. By the end of the war, the United States was in economic trouble again. The situation was similar to that of the nation after the American Revolution: trade was disrupted, the federal government was deep in debt, prices were high, and the country was flooded with paper money (this time issued by state banks) that was growing more worthless by the day. Even President Madison, despite his personal objections to a national bank, could see that something had to be done to restore economic order in the country. So on April 10, 1816, he signed a bill to create the Second Bank of the United States.

A BRIEF HISTORY OF US MONEY

Before the American Civil War (1861–1865), the US government did not issue paper money. The Constitution only granted the government the power to issue coins. The Continental Congress's paper money issued during the American Revolution had quickly grown worthless and had contributed to the young nation's economic problems. As a result, many Americans did not trust paper money. The founders preferred to base US currency on gold and silver coins. Since gold and silver were scarce, American-made coins were initially in short supply. Citizens were allowed to use either US-made coins or foreign ones.

Paper money continued to circulate. But banks—not the government—issued these banknotes. About sixteen

Only fifteen specimens of the 1804 dollar exist in the twenty-first century. Despite the date on the coin, none of them were made before the 1830s.

hundred different banks, each chartered by a US state, issued banknotes before the Civil War. These banknotes could be redeemed for specie, or gold and silver coins. Because so many different banknotes existed, they were easy to fake, and counterfeiting was common.

The National Bank Act of 1863, passed during the Civil War, created a system of banks chartered by the federal government instead of the states. It also created a single national currency of coins and paper money to be produced by the Department of the Treasury's Bureau of Engraving and Printing. US currency continued to be exchangeable for gold until 1933.

The government of Texas at Houston issued this twenty–dollar banknote in April 1838.

THE SECOND BANK OF THE UNITED STATES

The purpose of the Second Bank was essentially the same as that of the First Bank. But the Second Bank got off to a bad start. Its first two presidents served from 1816 to 1823. The first bank president, William Jones, lent too much money, then quickly changed his mind and restricted loans. A recession followed, interest rates and unemployment soared, and prices for farm crops sank. The second bank president, Langdon Cheves, tried to reverse the recession but made it worse by collecting banknotes issued by state banks and then presenting the notes for gold or silver coins, which bankrupted the state banks. The recession worsened into a depression. Many Americans blamed the bank for their troubles, and for good reason.

Nicholas Biddle (above) was much more successful at managing the Second Bank of the United States than his predecessors were.

In 1823 Nicholas Biddle took over management of the Second Bank of the United States. Biddle, unlike his predecessors, was a skilled manager. He had experience in banking and politics. He stabilized the amount of paper currency in circulation. Business activity expanded, and the American economy began to prosper again. The bank's reputation improved greatly, and it became successful.

When Jackson ran for president in 1828, the

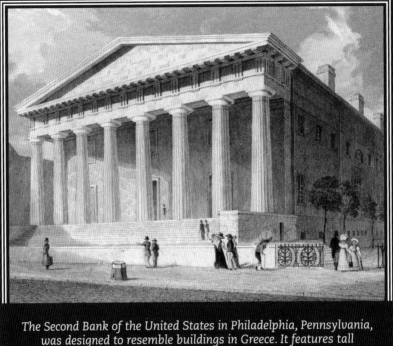

The Second Bank of the United States in Philadelphia, Pennsylvania, was designed to resemble buildings in Greece. It features tall columns, typical in Greek architecture.

Second Bank was not a campaign issue for either side. But it became clear in his first presidential address to Congress in 1829 that he was not a fan of the bank. At the end of this speech, he said, "The charter of the Bank of the United States expires in 1836, and its stock holders will most probably apply for a renewal of their privileges. . . . Both the constitutionality and the expediency of the law creating this bank are well questioned by a large portion of our fellow citizens, and it must be admitted by all that it has failed in the great end of establishing . . . uniform and sound currency."

Jackson believed that a national bank was unconstitutional and gave too much control over the nation's financial system to too few people, with too little public oversight. In addition, he had a strong personal dislike of banks. He felt that the bank, as

> Office of Bank U. States, Washington, *Aug 15ᵗʰ 18 32*
>
> PAY to *N. P. Trist* — — — or bearer,
> *one hundred* — — — dollars,
>
> *Andrew Jackson*
>
> *100* – DOLLS.   100
> 16394   100

Jackson wrote this check for one hundred dollars from the Bank of the United States in 1832, despite his distrust of banks.

a federal institution, trampled on states' rights. Further, more than twenty years earlier, Jackson had accepted paper money as payment for some land. When the buyers went bankrupt, Jackson's paper money became worthless. After that, he no longer trusted paper money. He believed that gold and silver coins were the only acceptable forms of currency, and that people should never borrow money. Since banks were the issuers of paper money and loans, Jackson was suspicious of all banks.

Biddle was not open to criticism about the bank. Instead, he looked for a way to circumvent Jackson's opposition. Senators Henry Clay and Daniel Webster advised Biddle to seek an early congressional recharter of the Second Bank—in 1832 instead of 1836. The bank had more supporters than opponents, in both the general public and in Congress. Because 1832 was a presidential election year, the men wagered that Jackson would not want to veto the recharter and make a campaign issue of it.

Biddle, Clay, and Webster were trying to force Jackson's hand with public pressure. They were daring him to oppose them. This was the same strategy Calhoun and the nullifiers had tried at the 1830 Jefferson dinner. The tactic didn't work any better for the Second Bank than it had for nullification. When Biddle's

supporters introduced the recharter bill, Jackson exclaimed to Van Buren, "The Bank is trying to kill me, Sir, but I shall kill it!"

When the recharter bill came through Congress, both chambers passed it—and as expected, Jackson vetoed it. In his veto message, Jackson said that the Second Bank was "unauthorized by the Constitution, subversive to the rights of States, and dangerous to the liberties of the people." And the veto held up in Congress, where there weren't enough votes to overturn it.

As promised, Jackson's bank veto became a major issue in the 1832 election. Although the Second Bank was indeed popular, Jackson's popularity was even stronger. He easily defeated his opponent, Henry Clay. Jackson interpreted his reelection as a request from the US people to destroy the Second Bank.

Whig Party members Daniel Webster (center) and Henry Clay (right), shown in this portrait with Jackson (left), supported the bank recharter.

THE BANK VETO

Jackson's bank veto was important for two reasons. First, it marked a turning point in the use of presidential veto power. Before Jackson, US presidents had rarely vetoed bills, and they'd done so only when they believed bills were unconstitutional. Jackson, by contrast, vetoed the bank bill not only because he believed it was unconstitutional (even though the US Supreme Court had already ruled that it was constitutional) but also for political reasons.

Second, Jackson's bank veto message cemented his popularity and assured his reelection in 1832. Here is a famous excerpt from Jackson's veto message:

> The rich and powerful too often bend the acts of government to their selfish purposes. Distinctions in society will always exist under every just government. Equality of talents, of education, or of wealth can not be produced by human institutions . . . but when the laws undertake to add to these natural and just advantages artificial distinctions, to grant titles, gratuities, and exclusive privileges, to make the rich richer and the potent more powerful, the humble members of society— the farmers, mechanics, and laborers—who have neither the time nor the means of securing like favors to themselves, have a right to complain of the injustice of their Government.

After the nullification crisis passed in 1833, Jackson ordered the federal government's deposits in the Second Bank to be moved to multiple state banks. This would shrink the Second Bank's size and power, until its charter expired in 1836. Biddle retaliated by cutting back on the granting of loans and calling for payment of existing loans. This tactic caused financial panic, which Biddle hoped would turn Americans against Jackson. Biddle was wrong. The people turned against him instead, because he'd proven Jackson's point that the Second Bank was meddling in politics and manipulating the financial system for its own benefit. In 1834 Congress voted to keep federal deposits in the state banks. When its charter expired, the Second Bank accepted a state charter from Pennsylvania and became a state bank.

This 1834 cartoon portrays Jackson as the champion of the common man against the moneyed interests of the Second Bank. In the center, Biddle (left) and Jackson (right) square off.

ASSASSINATION ATTEMPT

On January 30, 1835, Jackson became the first US president to experience an assassination attempt. On that day, Richard Lawrence, a mentally unstable, unemployed housepainter, was hiding as Jackson left a funeral. Lawrence believed that Jackson had denied him a job, thus preventing the government from paying him a large amount of money. With that money, Lawrence believed, he would assume his birthright as king of England.

Lawrence shot at Jackson. His gun's percussion cap exploded, but the gunpowder didn't ignite, and the bullet stayed put. Jackson jumped into action, beating his attacker with his walking stick. Lawrence pulled out another pistol and shot again, but that gun too misfired. By then others, including Congressman David (Davy) Crockett, had rushed to help Jackson.

Jackson believed that his enemies in the Whig Party, who opposed his closure of the Second Bank, had hired Lawrence. An investigation found that Lawrence was mentally ill and disgruntled but was not a paid assassin.

Richard Lawrence (above, left), an unemployed housepainter, attempted to assassinate Jackson on January 30, 1835.

THE AFTERMATH

Even after the Second Bank's demise, Jackson continued his attack on banking. He tried to force a return to gold and silver coins by issuing an executive order called the Specie Circular in 1836. This order required people to pay for government lands in gold and silver coins, not paper money, after August 15, 1836.

Meanwhile, the US economy spun into chaos. The state banks had grown fat with government funds and had been cut loose from the restraints of the powerful Second Bank. The state banks granted loans too freely, leading investors to spend wildly and unwisely.

That economic bubble burst in the Panic of 1837, just as Jackson left office. British banks, which had been investing heavily in US enterprises, stopped pumping money into the US economy so they could respond to their home country's financial problems. Once the British banks cut back on credit, so did the US banks. Jackson's Specie Circular worsened the credit crunch by forcing people to pay for land in gold and silver. The nation's economy sank into a depression that lasted well into the 1840s.

A general store customer looks with worry at the bill of money he owes during the Panic of 1837.

CHAPTER FIVE

WESTWARD EXPANSION AND AMERICAN INDIAN REMOVAL

In managing internal affairs, President Jackson maintained two goals. He wanted to protect the American people from corruption in their leaders and institutions, and he wanted to preserve the Union from division. But his actions were often heavy-handed, and the results of his efforts were mixed as can be seen in Jackson's handling of the federal bureaucracy, the American System, abolitionism, and the Second Bank. Jackson's handling of American Indian relations was similarly conflicted.

EUROPEAN SETTLERS AND AMERICAN INDIANS

In the early sixteenth century, when Europeans began exploring and colonizing the Americas, American Indians had already been living there for thousands of years. They had developed many diverse cultures and ways of life, from small nomadic groups of hunter-gatherers to permanent city dwellers, dependent on agriculture.

When the newcomers from Europe arrived, they brought foreign ideas, such as the Christian religion, money, and private ownership of land. They brought new tools, such as guns and plows. They also brought new diseases, such as smallpox, to which American Indians had no immunity. Smallpox spread easily, and it wiped out whole societies.

By the turn of the nineteenth century, European American settlers had been encroaching on the American Indians' homelands for three centuries. The growing population of white Americans wanted more room to build homes and farms and establish towns and industries. American Indians wanted to maintain their homelands and their autonomy as independent nations. At various times and places, American Indians had been both adapting to new economic and cultural systems and resisting their encroachment by force. The conflict continued, and ongoing years of violence sowed mistrust and fear.

SHARP KNIFE

As a young man and a new lawyer in 1787 and 1788, Andrew Jackson had traveled west from North Carolina to live in Tennessee—then the American frontier. Jackson was just one of many white people pouring into what was then called Indian country. On his journey west and during his travels around Tennessee, Jackson earned a reputation as being good at avoiding attacks from American Indians.

Jackson earned a different sort of reputation among members of the Creek Nation in the area. In 1812 the Creek divided into two main factions: one that wanted to maintain good relations with the United States and one that wanted to destroy US settlements. The latter group called itself the Red Sticks. This split led to a Creek civil war and brought numerous attacks by the Red Sticks on white newcomers. Jackson, then a Tennessee

"RESTORE TO US OUR COUNTRY AND WE SHALL BE ENEMIES NO LONGER"

The impasse between settlers and American Indians is apparent in the following excerpt from a 1793 letter to the US government from members of the Shawnee, Delaware (Lenape), and Miami nations of the Ohio River valley, who had been forced off their land by US settlements:

> **BROTHERS;—** Money, to us, is of no value, & to most of us unknown, and . . . no consideration whatever can induce us to sell the lands on which we get sustenance for our women and children. . . .

> You have talked to us about concessions. It appears strange that you should expect any from us, who have only been defending our just Rights against your invasion; We want Peace; Restore to us our Country and we shall be Enemies no longer. . . .

> We desire you to consider Brothers, that our only demand, is the peaceable possession of a small part of our once great Country. Look back and view the lands from whence we have been driven to this spot, we can retreat no further, because the country behind hardly affords food for its present inhabitants. And we have therefore resolved, to leave our bones in this small space, to which we are now confined.

militia officer, cultivated allies among the Creek who wanted to keep peace with the United States and joined in their fight against the Red Sticks. The Creek War carried on through 1813 and early 1814. Jackson's troops nearly starved and had heavy casualties. The terrible conditions led Jackson's soldiers to mutiny, but Jackson faced them down and kept his troops together. Eventually the Red Sticks were defeated.

Jackson was responsible for negotiating a peace treaty with the Creek. President Madison's administration had sent guidelines instructing Jackson to obtain an unspecified amount

Jackson (above, on horseback) had to face down a mutiny because living conditions for his soldiers were so terrible during the Creek War.

LYNCOYA

After a Red Stick massacre of at least 250 American soldiers, civilians, and enslaved people at Fort Mims, near modern Mobile, Alabama, Jackson marched his Tennessee militia into the area. To avenge the deaths at Fort Mims, he sent about 1,000 of his soldiers to Tallushatchee, a Creek village where a Red Stick war party was staying. The militia destroyed the village and killed nearly 200 Creek warriors. Davy Crockett, who was part of Jackson's militia, said, "We shot 'em down like dogs."

Afterward, soldiers found a baby holding onto his dead mother. When Jackson learned about this, he took the boy into his care, eventually sending him home to the Hermitage. Jackson named the boy Lyncoya, and he and Rachel raised him as their own son. Lyncoya Jackson died of a lung disease in 1828, still in his teens.

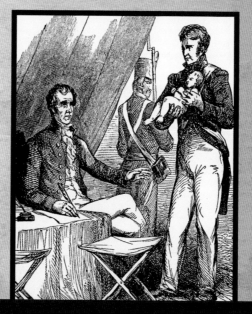

Lyncoya, an orphaned Creek Indian, is presented to Andrew Jackson (seated) after the Battle of Horseshoe Bend.

of land, a guarantee of safe travel through the area for US citizens, the right to establish military posts, and the surrender of what the government considered Creek instigators. Jackson thought the terms should be harsher. A resident of the area himself, he agreed with other local white residents that a very large amount of land was necessary to ensure the safety of US citizens. Further, a growing southern population and an expanding cotton industry, dependent on the labor of enslaved African Americans, pressed for more land.

Jackson demanded half of the Creek's territory: 22 million acres (9 million hectares), about 60 percent of modern Alabama and 20 percent of modern Georgia. Most of the Creek who would suffer under these terms had been US allies. Even so, he told the Creek either they could sign the treaty and prove their friendship or flee to Spanish- or British- held lands in Florida.

All but one of the Red Stick chiefs fled to Florida. With no other viable choice, the remaining Creek chiefs, most of whom had been US allies, signed the treaty. For Jackson's harsh terms and unwillingness to negotiate, the Creek gave him a new nickname: Sharp Knife. In a letter to Rachel, Andrew Jackson called his dealings with the Creek "a disagreeable business." He told her, "I know your humanity would feel for them."

JACKSON'S VIEWS ON AMERICAN INDIANS

Jackson's actions reflected his overall attitude toward American Indians. He was willing to cooperate with American Indians when alliance seemed practical. But he viewed them as children who needed guidance. He believed that American Indian society was inferior to white society and that white leaders should decide what was best for both groups.

By the time Andrew Jackson became president, he'd had a lot of experience with the westward expansion of white settlements

in North America. He had been a strong and steady advocate for American Indian removal and relocation ever since he moved to Tennessee. His main goal was to further the growth of the United States and the success of its white citizens. Jackson was a key negotiator in nine treaties signed from 1814 to 1824. Under pressure, American Indians signed treaties ceding, or yielding, pieces of present-day Florida, Georgia, North Carolina, Alabama, Mississippi, Tennessee, and Kentucky in exchange for protection from white harassment.

Jackson made his philosophy clear in his first address to Congress in 1829. He acknowledged that white people had mistreated, squeezed out, and ultimately decimated whole societies. White society had caused further problems by establishing self-governing American Indian territories inside US states. The tribes in these territories were arguing with the states about who had authority over their lands. It was too late, Jackson said, to undo what had already been done. But it was not too late to do better with the situation that remained.

INDIAN REMOVAL ACT

One year later, Jackson proposed a bill he hoped would resolve the United States' conflict with American Indians. The Indian Removal Act would give him the power to designate new American Indian lands west of the Mississippi River, which defined the boundary of existing US states at that time. It also would give him the power to negotiate removal treaties with nations east of the Mississippi. These treaties would exchange the western lands for the eastern ones and pay for the relocation of American Indians to the new territories, where they would exist as independent nations. If they stayed in their original homelands, Jackson said, the federal government would not protect them and they would become subject to the laws of

the states where they resided. In Georgia, for example, they would not be able to own property. Given the conditions, some American Indians did favor moving to new lands to remain self-governing, rather than becoming subjects of the US government and assimilating into the dominant culture.

Jackson's Indian Removal bill was met with a strong negative reaction from some sections of white society. Christian ministers and women, many of whom were or would become abolitionists, were the driving forces behind an anti-removal movement. Activists included Catharine Beecher, whose sister Harriet Beecher Stowe would write the influential antislavery novel *Uncle Tom's Cabin*. Beecher recruited women to send petitions protesting removal to Congress. This was the first such national campaign by US women. Society did not grant women political power, but Beecher framed the anti-removal issue as a moral, humanitarian one, proper to the concerns of women. It was wrong, she wrote, "that [American Indians] are to have their lands torn from them, and to be driven into western wilds and to final annihilation [because

Catharine Beecher (above) began a letter-writing campaign to Congress protesting the government's removal of American Indians.

their] fertile and valuable [lands are] demanded by the whites as their own possessions." She and other activists still considered white culture superior to American Indian culture. They supported educating American Indians about Christian traditions instead of removing them.

Sequoyah invented eighty-six characters for writing the Cherokee language.

The vote on the bill in the House of Representatives was tight, 102–97, but Jackson pressured Congress, and they passed the Indian Removal Act in May 1830. In his annual message to Congress at the end of that year, Jackson said removal was for the American Indians' own good.

> Speedy removal . . . will separate the Indians from immediate contact with settlements of whites; free them from the power of the States; enable them to pursue happiness in their own way and under their own rude institutions; . . . and perhaps cause them gradually, under the protection of the Government and through the influence of good counsels, to cast off their savage habits and become an interesting, civilized, and Christian community. . . .
>
> The policy of the General Government toward the red man is . . . generous. He is unwilling to submit to the laws of the States and mingle with their population. To save him . . . , the General Government kindly offers him a new home, and proposes to pay the whole expense of his removal and settlement.

THE FLOURISHING CHEROKEE NATION

By the time of Jackson's presidency, some native nations were already living in the kinds of societies of which Jackson himself said he approved. The Cherokee Nation, for instance, along with the Creek, Choctaw, Chickasaw, and Seminole, had responded creatively to the coming of white society. The five were known to white society as the Five Civilized Tribes.

The Cherokee had long flourished in northwest Georgia and surrounding areas. As treaties restricted their hunting lands, the Cherokee adapted. They built permanent towns and farms and set up thriving businesses trading with white people. This nation of more than thirteen thousand people established a Cherokee National Council, which set up a legal system and adopted a constitution. Some Cherokee attended Christian-run schools, adopted the Christian religion, and married white people. A small minority—mostly people with white parentage—even bought enslaved African Americans to perform the hard labor of growing cotton, like the white planters around them.

In 1821 a Cherokee man named Sequoyah introduced a system he had invented for writing the Cherokee language. A newspaper followed, the *Cherokee Phoenix*, which published articles in Cherokee and English. In 1824 a Cherokee delegation to the white people's government in Washington, DC, explained they would not give up any more land. "The Cherokee are not foreigners, but original inhabitants of America," they said, "and the limits of their territory are defined by the treaties which they have made with the Government of the United States."

THE TRAIL OF TEARS

Not only did the Indian Removal Act force people off their land, but it caused widespread misery and death. In 1832 groups of the Chickasaw, Choctaw, Creek, and Seminole who lived in Mississippi, Alabama, and Georgia signed treaties with the US government and moved. Meanwhile, some members of all four groups stayed behind. But the US government did not deliver on its promise to protect the American Indians who stayed. Through the 1830s, land-hungry European newcomers harassed them relentlessly and eventually forced out many of the remaining American Indians. Thousands died along the way west due to outbreaks of cholera, starvation, bitter cold, and exhaustion. The government had broken another promise of the Indian Removal Act—that of paying the costs of migration and ensuring supplies and safe travel.

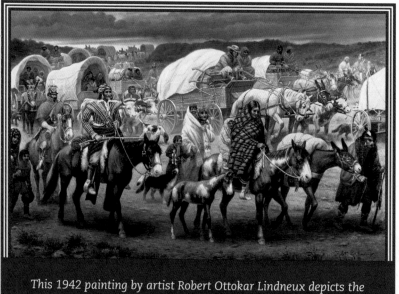

This 1942 painting by artist Robert Ottokar Lindneux depicts the Trail of Tears.

The Cherokee of Georgia resisted removal by legal means. In 1835 a minority faction signed a treaty with the US government. Despite protests from the majority, the US Supreme Court ratified the treaty in 1836. The government gave the Cherokee two years to move. Only about two thousand did. About sixteen thousand Cherokee remained on their land in 1838. So the government sent seven thousand soldiers to remove the Cherokee. The soldiers rounded them up at gunpoint with no possessions and force-marched them west to modern-day Oklahoma. About four thousand Cherokee men, women, and children starved, froze, sickened and died, or were murdered by hostile white people along the 1,200-mile (1,931 km) route. The Cherokee later named this route the Place Where They Cried, and it became known as the Trail of Tears.

The Seminole fiercely resisted removal. Those who didn't move west fled to Florida. Their armed resistance to US troops

Seminole Indians attack a US fort in Florida in December 1835.

Barracks and tents house soldiers at a US military fort during the Second Seminole War in Florida in 1835.

attempting to remove them led to the Second Seminole War (1835–1842). The First Seminole War (1817–1818) had been fought when Andrew Jackson and his troops invaded Florida after the War of 1812. The US military, at the cost of $20 million, defeated the Seminole. The military forced most of the Seminole to relocate west at this point, although about five hundred stayed in Florida. They fled into the swampy, alligator-infested Everglades, where most white people didn't venture. By isolating themselves in this area, they maintained their society into modern times.

Northern states practiced removal too. The brief 1832 Black Hawk War in Illinois and Wisconsin, for instance, pushed thousands of native peoples off their lands, opening the way for white settlement.

US government treaties promised that the new western lands would remain in American Indian hands forever. As the country continued to expand westward, however, the government repeatedly broke those treaties, and American Indian territory continued to dwindle.

CHAPTER SIX

FOREIGN AFFAIRS AND JACKSON'S LEGACY

The social and economic events taking place in the United States during Andrew Jackson's presidency were dramatic ones. Jackson faced a variety of international concerns too. He could be a careful diplomat when he chose to be. His dealings with Great Britain, France, and Mexico are good examples of this ability.

GREAT BRITAIN

After the American Revolution ended, Great Britain began restricting trade between the United States and the British West Indies, or the British colonies in the Caribbean islands. These restrictions took various forms. At times, Great Britain banned US imports outright. At other times, the British imposed high tariffs, banned certain goods, or set limits on the amount of imports.

The United States wanted to trade freely with the British West Indies, as it had done when it was under British rule. Exports of products such as flour, corn, and wood to these islands made up about 10 percent of total US exports, so this trade was important to the young US economy. British leaders, however, viewed the US desire for free trade in the British West Indies with resentment. From their perspective, it seemed that the United States wanted to keep the benefits of being part of the British Empire after having left it violently.

The disagreement between the two nations dragged on into the nineteenth century. Even after the War of 1812 ended, Great Britain was still restricting imports from the United States. So the United States retaliated against Great Britain by restricting imports from the British West Indies with three separate acts in 1818, 1820, and 1823. During John Quincy Adams' administration (1824–1829), the British tried to resolve this dispute, but Adams did not respond, and trade between the British West Indies and the United States remained stalled.

After Jackson took office as president, he appointed Louis McLane his ambassador to Great Britain. McLane pointed out that Jackson's election offered an opportunity to break the trade deadlock. The administration could

Louis McLane, the US ambassador to Great Britain from 1829 to 1831

paint Jackson's defeat of Adams as a national rejection of Adams's foreign policy. With that in mind, the British might consider reopening trade negotiations.

Jackson liked this idea. He was eager for diplomatic success. So he encouraged Congress to pass a bill authorizing the repeal of the retaliatory acts of 1818, 1820, and 1823 as soon as Great Britain allowed US ships to import and export goods from the British West Indies with the same terms that British ships enjoyed. Congress passed the bill in 1830. The British responded just as McLane predicted.

GREASING THE WHEELS

Jackson had never had warm feelings toward the British. He'd lost his family in the American Revolution and had fought the British both as a boy soldier and again as an officer in the War of 1812. But he understood the difference between a soldier's and a president's job. His cordial words about Great Britain in his first message to Congress were indeed a new approach for him—but they were perfectly logical. He was greasing the wheels of diplomatic negotiation. "With Great Britain, alike distinguished in peace and war," Jackson wrote, "we may look forward to years of peaceful, honorable, and elevated competition. Every thing in the condition and history of the two nations is calculated to inspire sentiments of mutual respect and to carry conviction to the minds of both that it is their policy to preserve the most cordial relations."

FRANCE

While the United States danced delicately with Great Britain over trade issues, it was also wrestling with France about the settlement of old financial scores dating back to the Napoleonic Wars (1803–1815). These were a series of conflicts that began in 1799, in which France and Great Britain fought each other (and an ever-shifting set of allies) for economic and political dominance in Europe. During these wars, France had looted US ships trading with Great Britain.

By the time Jackson became president, the United States had been trying for more than a decade to get France to pay for its damages to US shipping. In 1831, during Jackson's first term, France signed a treaty with the United States. Under this treaty, France would repay the United States in six installments. In his 1831 address to Congress, Jackson proudly explained his satisfaction with the treaty, saying that "a source of irritation will be stopped that has for so many years in some degree alienated from each other two nations who . . . ought to cherish the most friendly relations."

Jackson's satisfaction with France was short-lived. The first payment was due in late 1832 but didn't arrive as expected. In early 1833, US officials discovered that the payments required appropriation by France's Chamber of Deputies—an act similar to the US Congress setting aside money for a specific use—and that the chamber had not provided it. Jackson sent an emissary to France to demand payment, but the chamber did nothing until a year later. Then, in early 1834, the chamber defeated the appropriation bill.

King Louis Philippe I of France and his ministers assured Jackson that they would press the chamber to appropriate the money. But in the summer of 1834, the chamber announced it would not address the issue until the winter session of 1835. At

the end of 1834, Jackson's frustration was evident in his annual address to Congress. He suggested that the United States should take what France owed US citizens. Continued delay, he said, "is not to be tolerated. . . . The laws of nations provide a remedy for such occasions . . . where one nation owes another a liquidated debt which it refuses or neglects to pay the aggrieved party may seize on the property belonging to the other, its citizens or subjects, sufficient to pay the debt."

Throughout 1835 the stalemate between France and the United States grew tense. France was insulted by Jackson's statements to Congress. It called its ambassador home from the United States and demanded an explanation of Jackson's statements before it would pay. Jackson refused, saying that such a demand was insulting, and called the US ambassador home from France. Both countries began preparing their militaries for conflict. In late 1835, Jackson addressed Congress again, defending his position but also saying that he had never meant to threaten or insult the government of France.

British intermediaries encouraged French officials to take Jackson's 1835 statement to Congress as an apology. They did. France also paid its debt. This long-awaited resolution elevated the

King Louis Philippe I of France

standing of the United States in international relations. The rest of the world began to view the United States as a nation worthy of respect, rather than a weak newcomer.

MEXICO

A few years before Jackson became president, circumstances to the south and west of the United States underwent a dramatic change. The Spanish colony of New Spain, which included most of present-day Mexico and the entire US Southwest, gained independence from Spain in 1821. The new country became the Republic of Mexico in 1824.

Meanwhile, US settlers were pouring into Texas, then a northern province of Mexico. In 1820, when Mexico was still New Spain, American citizen Moses Austin had gotten Spain's permission to establish a US colony in Texas. Spain agreed to Austin's plan because Texas was sparsely settled—only about thirty-five hundred people lived there—and the government needed help from new settlers to develop the land. In addition, the government believed that offering legal settlement to Americans would discourage illegal settlement, which was causing problems in eastern Texas. By 1830 about sixteen thousand Americans lived in Texas, which had become a part of the Republic of Mexico. Americans made up 80 percent of the population of northern Texas, but people of Mexican heritage still made up a majority of Texas's population.

The Mexican government grew uncomfortable with the large US population in Texas. The Americans refused to assimilate into Mexican society and did most of their business with one another and the United States. Relations between US settlers and native Mexicans in Texas were tense. Mexican authorities worried that the United States would start a revolution in Texas and then acquire the area as a US state. So Mexico ended US

immigration, restricted trade with the United States, and beefed up security in Texas. The Americans didn't like these measures, of course, and they were even more unhappy when in 1834 General Antonio López de Santa Anna overthrew the democratic government, made himself dictator, and did away with Mexico's state governments.

In 1835 US colonists in Texas drew up a constitution and assembled their own government. Some of them began to take up arms against Mexican rule. By spring of 1836, a revolution was under way, led by Jackson's old Tennessee friend Sam Houston, with the help of volunteers from the southern United States. The Americans surprised Santa Anna's forces and captured the general on April 21. On April 22, the Americans forced Santa Anna

General Antonio López de Santa Anna

to sign a treaty giving Texas independence. Most Mexican Texans, now second-class citizens according to the Texas constitution, fled. Shortly thereafter, Texans voted nearly unanimously to become a part of the United States.

Andrew Jackson had always seen the US-Mexico border as problematic. He wanted the United States to annex Texas to improve the security of the Southwest. At the beginning of his presidency, he tried to

REMEMBER THE ALAMO!

In mid-1835, Americans captured the city of San Antonio and its Mexican military headquarters, a fortified mission called the Alamo. In early 1836, word reached the Americans in Texas that General Antonio López de Santa Anna was marching north with seven thousand soldiers to squash the rebellion. When Sam Houston heard the news, he ordered Americans to abandon San Antonio.

About 200 rebels—mostly Americans but also including a few Mexican allies—chose to gather at the Alamo to defend San Antonio. After a twelve-day siege, Santa Anna's soldiers scaled the walls of the Alamo and overwhelmed the rebels. About 190 defenders died. Santa Anna's troops stacked the bodies, poured oil on them, and set them on fire.

Although the Battle of the Alamo ended in defeat for the rebels, it became a strong motivator. Thereafter, the rallying cry for Texans fighting for independence, was Remember the Alamo!

Fall of the Alamo, *an illustration from 1896*

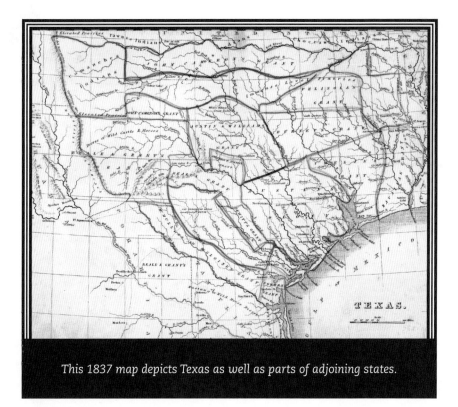

This 1837 map depicts Texas as well as parts of adjoining states.

buy Texas from Mexico for $5 million. But he bungled the job by assigning negotiations to Anthony Butler. Butler was impatient, clumsy, and corrupt. His dealings in Mexico contributed to the Mexican government's mistrust of the United States and US settlers in the early 1830s, which later led to the Texas Revolution.

When Texas declared independence in 1836 and appealed to Jackson for recognition and annexation, Jackson still wanted to acquire the state. But the domestic situation had changed. Slavery had become a hotly debated issue, and slavery was legal in Texas. Jackson was worried that acquiring Texas as a slave state would upset the precarious balance of slave and nonslave states and stir up both abolitionists and secessionists. The debate would strain the Union, divide the Democratic Party, and put Van Buren's

chance of election as Jackson's successor in danger. Jackson waited to recognize Texas as an independent nation until the final days of his presidency in March 1837, after Van Buren had been elected. He left the question of annexation to Congress, which eventually approved annexation of Texas as the twenty-eighth state in 1845.

JACKSON'S LEGACY

After Andrew Jackson handed over the presidential reins to Martin Van Buren, he headed home to the Hermitage. Throughout his presidency, he'd been longing for a return to a quiet, private life. But once he got his wish, he apparently missed politics. He kept in close touch with Van Buren, showering him with advice for his presidency and assistance in his bid for reelection. He stayed involved in politics even after Van Buren lost the election of 1840, particularly by supporting US efforts to annex Texas under presidents John Tyler and James Polk. By that time, he was in his seventies. His body was wearing out from age and the strain of many injuries and illnesses. He died at home on June 8, 1845, at the age of seventy-eight.

This photo of Jackson in 1845 at seventy-eight years old was taken months before his death.

Andrew and Rachel Jackson never had any biological children. They were, however, devoted parents to a large family of adopted and fostered children.

In 1808 Rachel's brother and sister-in-law had twin sons. The Jacksons adopted one of the babies and named him Andrew Jr. In 1813 the Jacksons adopted the Creek baby Lyncoya, and the two boys grew up side by side. After Lyncoya's death and Jackson's election to the presidency in 1828, Andrew Jr. took over management of the Hermitage.

Andrew Jackson served as guardian to several other

children. In Jackson's time, it was common for the courts to appoint a male guardian for any child whose father died—even if the child's mother was still living.

When Jackson's brother-in-law Samuel died in 1804, Jackson became guardian to Samuel's three sons, including Andrew Jackson Donelson.

Andrew Jackson Donelson, President Jackson's nephew and ward

These boys lived part-time at the Hermitage. Jackson took a special interest in Andrew Jackson Donelson, making sure he attended the US Military Academy at West Point and law school afterward. Andrew Jackson Donelson became President Jackson's personal secretary, and his wife, Emily Donelson, served as his White House hostess.

Jackson also was the guardian of the four children of General Edward Butler, who was a hero of the American Revolution. The four lived part-time at the Hermitage, like the Donelson boys.

Finally, Rachel and Andrew Jackson adopted the orphaned grandson of Rachel's sister Catherine. The boy, Andrew Jackson Hutchings, born in 1812, lived full-time at the Hermitage. He grew up and attended school alongside Andrew Jackson Jr. and Lyncoya.

Emily Donelson, Andrew Jackson Donelson's wife, served as the White House hostess.

Andrew Jackson died at the Hermitage on June 8, 1845.

Jackson's impact on US politics did not end with his death. His legacy has been extensive, long lasting, and quite complicated. While many historians classify Jackson as one of the United States' most important presidents, none of these scholars has been able to boil down Jackson's legacy to one or two accomplishments, issues, or philosophies.

Several of President Jackson's efforts had a strong or immediate impact or led to later events. For example, Jackson's well-organized campaign machine soon became a new political party—the Democratic Party, which continues into modern times. When Jackson assumed office in 1829, he established a spoils system for federal bureaucrats that is still in place. During his two terms as president, Jackson boldly defied both nullifiers and abolitionists, thereby enshrining the Union in a way that no president before him had and that many who followed him

would emulate. Through his vetoes of transportation subsidies and the Second Bank of the United States, Jackson triggered a transformation in presidential veto power away from strictly constitutional concerns toward more political ones. His death blow to the Second Bank led directly to an economic crash. Jackson also pushed through Congress the Indian Removal Act, with tragic repercussions for American Indians. And in Jackson's diplomatic dealings with Great Britain and France, he established

Jackson's tomb at the Hermitage

The Andrew Jackson monument, erected after Jackson's death, is across the street from the White House in Washington, DC.

the United States as a world power on the same footing with great powers in Europe.

These actions of Jackson are important, but they aren't grand enough to explain why Jackson remains a prominent name among US presidents. Many historians suggest that Jackson's prominence is more about who he was than what he did. In other words, Jackson has remained important to Americans because he is a symbol of American democracy. His rise from poverty to the presidency showed for the first time that in the United States, one's background can be less important than one's ambition. In Jackson's age, legal barriers held back women and people of color from full participation in democracy. The example of Jackson's rise has challenged the nation to remove barriers for Americans from all backgrounds.

JACKSON'S FAREWELL ADDRESS

In his farewell address to Congress on March 6, 1837, Jackson expressed these democratic ideals for which he would be remembered:

> The planter, the farmer, the mechanic, and the laborer all know that their success depends upon their own industry and economy. . . . These classes of society form the great body of the people of the United States; they are the bone and sinew of the country—men who love liberty and desire nothing but equal rights and equal laws.

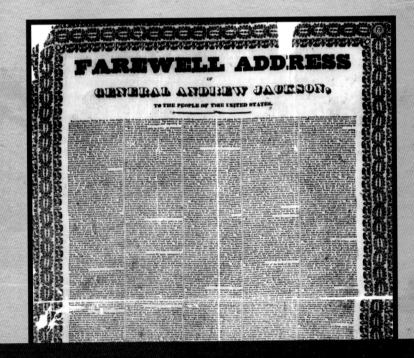

Jackson's 1837 farewell address, printed on silk

Jackson's rise to the presidency was somewhat unexpected. The US Constitution certainly allowed someone from his background to become president, but no one had yet achieved it. All Jackson's predecessors had come from wealthy and powerful families. Jackson, by contrast, was born into a poor immigrant family, and he was raised by a single, working mother. He received only a basic education, and his academic performance was unimpressive. He did not have the dignified heritage or manners of those who'd come before him. His marriage was considered scandalous. Jackson's personality was passionate, and his behavior was sometimes wild. But he was extremely hardworking, tough, confident, and unwilling to accept defeat. His rise to the presidency was a vivid example of what was, and would be, possible in the United States.

TIMELINE

1767	Andrew Jackson is born on March 15 in the Waxhaws region of the British Carolina colony.
1780	Andrew Jackson and his brother Robert join the patriot forces fighting in the American Revolution.
1788	In October, Jackson arrives in Tennessee, where he settles, begins a law practice, and meets Rachel Donelson Robards.
1791	Andrew and Rachel Jackson marry.
1794	The couple remarry after learning their first marriage was invalid.
1796	Tennessee becomes a state, due partly to Jackson's efforts.
1802	Jackson accepts his first military position, as major general of Tennessee's militia.
1812–1815	Jackson serves as an officer in the War of 1812, earns a reputation as a skilled and tough leader, and gains the nickname Old Hickory.
1824	Jackson runs for the US presidency and wins the most popular votes but not a majority. The House of Representatives elects John Quincy Adams in what Jackson calls a "corrupt bargain."
1828	Jackson runs for president again and wins. His wife, Rachel, dies, due partly to the stress of Jackson's campaign. Congress passes a high tariff rate that southerners call the Tariff of Abominations.
1829	Jackson establishes the spoils system. The Eaton Affair begins.
1830	Jackson initiates and pushes through Congress the Indian Removal Act. Jackson's administration reopens trade with the British West Indies.
1831	Jackson's administration signs a treaty with France for payment of long-overdue damages to US ships during the Napoleonic Wars.
1832	Congress passes a new tariff rate that isn't low enough to satisfy southerners, and South Carolina declares it null, feeding fears of secession. Jackson vetoes a bill meant to recharter the Second Bank of the United States.

1833   Congress passes the Compromise Tariff, and the nullification crisis passes.

1835   Richard Lawrence tries to assassinate Jackson but fails. France starts paying the damages it owes the United States. The Texas Revolution begins.

1836   Congress passes a gag rule prohibiting any discussion of slavery. The Texas Revolution ends, and Texas becomes an independent nation.

1837   Jackson leaves office. The economy begins to crash, partly as a result of his economic policies.

1838   The forced migration of the Cherokee known as the Trail of Tears, one direct result of Jackson's American Indian policy, begins. It ends in misery and death for thousands of Cherokee people.

1845   Jackson dies on June 8. Texas becomes a US state on December 29.

SOURCE NOTES

7   Steve Ember, "Andrew Jackson Leaves Office; Martin Van Buren Becomes President," Voice of America, March 20, 2014, http://m .learningenglish.voanews.com/a/andrew-jackson-van-buren /1775693.html.

11 Paul S. Vickery, *Jackson: The Iron-Willed Commander* (Nashville: Thomas Nelson, 2012), 5.

14 Ibid., 11.

15 Andrew Jackson, *The Papers of Andrew Jackson, vol. 1, 1770–1803,* Knoxville: University of Tennessee Press, 1980, 12.

20 Vickery, *Jackson,* 62.

23 "American President: Andrew Jackson; Campaigns and Elections," Miller Center, University of Virginia, accessed October 13, 2014, http://millercenter.org/president/biography/jackson-campaigns -and-elections.

25 Vickery, *Jackson,* 194.

25 Daniel Walker Howe, *What Hath God Wrought: The Transformation of America, 1815–1848* (Oxford: Oxford University Press, 2007), 328.

27 H. W. Brands, *Andrew Jackson: His Life and Times* (New York: Doubleday, 2005), 418.

30 "Bill of Rights," National Archives and Records Administration, March 4, 1789, accessed October 30, 2014, http://www.archives .gov/exhibits/charters/bill_of_rights_transcript.html.

31 Brands, *Andrew Jackson,* 417–418.

31 Ibid., 420.

34 Margaret Bayard Smith, "The Rise of Jacksonian Democracy: Eyewitness Accounts," White House Historical Association Classroom, January 1, 1829, accessed November 5, 2014, http:// www.whitehousehistory.org/teacher-resources/the-rise-of -jacksonian-democracy-eyewitness-accounts.

41–42 Andrew Jackson, "No. 26. Respecting the Nullifying Laws of South Carolina. Proclamation by Andrew Jackson, President of the United States," Library of Congress, December 10, 1832, accessed November 7, 2014, http://memory.loc.gov/cgi-bin/ampage?collId=llsl&fileName=011/llsl011.db&recNum=826.

44 Brands, *Andrew Jackson*, 477.

44 Vickery, *Jackson*, 195.

47 Harriet Martineau, *Retrospect of Western Travel*, 1838, in Daniel Walker Howe, *What Hath God Wrought: The Transformation of America, 1815–1848* (Oxford: Oxford University Press, 2007), n.p.

49 Independence Hall Association, "Jackson vs. Clay and Calhoun," ushistory.org, accessed November 7, 2014, http://www.ushistory.org/us/24e.asp.

53 Andrew Jackson, "First Annual Message, December 8, 1829," The American Presidency Project, accessed November 11, 2014, http://www.presidency.ucsb.edu/ws/?pid=29471.

55 "The War against the Bank," ushistory.org, accessed November 12, 2014, http://www.ushistory.org/us/24d.asp.

55 "Conflict with the Executive: The Bank War," National Archives, accessed November 12, 2014, http://www.archives.gov/exhibits/treasures_of_congress/text/page9_text.html.

56 Daniel Feller, "King Andrew and the Bank," *Humanities* 29, no. 1 (January/February 2008), http://www.neh.gov/humanities/2008/januaryfebruary/feature/king-andrew-and-the-bank.

62 "Negotiations between the Western Indian Confederacy & U.S. Commissioners on the Issue of the Ohio River as the Boundary of Indian Lands, August 1793," in *The Correspondence of Lieut. Governor John Graves Simcoe*, vols. 1–2 (Toronto: Ontario Historical Society, 1923–1924), accessed November 17, 2014, http://nationalhumanitiescenter.org/pds/livingrev/expansion/text6/negotiations.pdf.

64   Amanda Macias and Gus Lubin, "200 Years Ago, Davy Crockett and Andrew Jackson Won a Battle at Tallushatchee," *Business Insider*, November 3, 2013, http://www.businessinsider.com /battle-at-tallushatchee-2013-10.

65   Vickery, *Jackson,* 110.

67–68   Catharine Beecher, "Circular Addressed to the Benevolent Ladies of the U. States," December 25, 1829, in Theda Purdue and Michael D. Green, eds., *The Cherokee Removal: A Brief History with Documents*, 2nd ed. (Boston: Bedford, 2015), available online at Digital History, accessed November 16, 2015, http://www .digitalhistory.uh.edu/active_learning/explorations/indian _removal/removal_teacher.cfm.

68   Andrew Jackson, "Transcript of President Andrew Jackson's Message to Congress 'On Indian Removal' (1830)," Our Documents, accessed November 19, 2014, http://www .ourdocuments.gov/doc.php?flash=true&doc=25&page =transcript.

69   Howe, *What Hath God Wrought,* 345–346.

76   Andrew Jackson, "First Annual Message."

77   Andrew Jackson, "Third Annual Message, December 6, 1831," The American Presidency Project, accessed December 4, 2014, http:// www.presidency.ucsb.edu/ws/?pid=29473.

78   Andrew Jackson, "Sixth Annual Message, December 1, 1834," The American Presidency Project, accessed December 4, 2014, http:// www.presidency.ucsb.edu/ws/?pid=29476.

89   Andrew Jackson, "Farewell Address, March 4, 1837," The American Presidency Project, accessed November 14, 2015, http://www .presidency.ucsb.edu/ws/?pid=67087.

GLOSSARY

abolitionist: in the nineteenth-century United States, a person who wanted to end slavery

administration: the officials in the executive branch of government, responsible for carrying out the nation's laws

bureaucracy: a system of government officials

cabinet: a group of people whose job is to advise the head of a government, such as a president

colony: a territory belonging to or controlled by a nation outside the territory's borders

constitution: the basic beliefs and laws of a nation or state that establish the powers and duties of the government and guarantee certain rights to the people in it

depression: a period of low economic activity with high unemployment

export: to send goods for sale to another country

import: to receive goods for sale from another country

infrastructure: a system of public works such as roads, bridges, canals, and buildings

Loyalist: during the American Revolution, someone who wanted the thirteen North American colonies to remain under British rule

militia: a group of citizens with some military training who are called into action only in an emergency

nullification: an act of cancellation, specifically a state blocking or attempting to cancel the enforcement within its territory of a federal law of the United States

patriot: during the American Revolution, someone who wanted the thirteen North American colonies to gain independence from British rule

revenue: money earned

tariff: taxes a government places on imported goods

SELECTED BIBLIOGRAPHY

American History: Pre-Columbian to the New Millennium. ushistory.org. Accessed December 1, 2015. http://www.ushistory.org.

"Andrew Jackson (1767–1845)." Miller Center, University of Virginia. Accessed December 1, 2015. http://millercenter.org/president/jackson.

Brands, H. W. *Andrew Jackson: His Life and Times.* New York: Doubleday, 2005.

"Economic Education." Federal Reserve Bank of Philadelphia. Accessed December 1, 2015. http://philadelphiafed.org/publications/economic -education.

Howe, Daniel Walker. *What Hath God Wrought: The Transformation of America, 1815–1848.* Oxford: Oxford University Press, 2007.

Mintz, S., and S. McNeil. "Jacksonian Democracy." Digital History. Accessed December 1, 2015. http://www.digitalhistory.uh.edu/era .cfm?eraID=5&smtID=2.

Remini, Robert V. *Andrew Jackson and the Course of American Freedom.* Baltimore: Johns Hopkins University Press, 1981.

Vickery, Paul S. *Jackson: The Iron-Willed Commander.* Nashville: Thomas Nelson, 2012.

Widmer, Ted. "The Age of Jackson." The Gilder Lehrman Institute of American History. Accessed December 1, 2015. http://www.gilderlehrman .org/history-by-era/national-expansion-and-reform-1815-1860/age -jackson.

Woolley, John T., and Gerhard Peters. The American Presidency Project. Accessed December 1, 2015. http://www.presidency.ucsb.edu/.

FURTHER INFORMATION

Africans in America: PBS
http://www.pbs.org/wgbh/aia/home.html
Loaded with historical documents, this website presents the history of Africans in America as well as related issues such as the abolitionist movement, westward expansion, and American Indian removal.

The American Presidency: Smithsonian Institution
http://americanhistory.si.edu/presidency/home.html
This online exhibit of the Smithsonian Institution's Museum of American History delves into the personal, political, social, and historical aspects of the American presidency, from Revolutionary America to modern times.

Barden, Cindy, and Maria Backus. *Westward Expansion and Migration.* Quincy, IL: Mark Twain Media, 2011.
Readers explore history, geography, and social studies related to US westward growth. This book includes information about the Trail of Tears and much more.

Bausum, Ann. *Our Country's Presidents: All You Need to Know about the Presidents, from George Washington to Barack Obama.* Washington, DC: National Geographic, 2013.
This comprehensive guide presents the leaders of the United States. It describes how each president has left a unique mark on the nation and on the lives of the American people.

Behnke, Alison. *A Timeline History of the Trail of Tears.* Minneapolis: Lerner Publications, 2016. Learn about the Cherokee Nation's forced removal from their homeland under Andrew Jackson's Indian Removal Act of 1830. This book tracks the events and turning points that led to this dark and tragic time in US history.

Hollar, Sherman. *Andrew Jackson.* New York: Rosen, 2012.
This book introduces readers to Andrew Jackson, the first leader from west of the Appalachians and the first to win office by directly appealing to the American people, rather than relying on a political party.

Mapping History: University of Oregon
http://mappinghistory.uoregon.edu
At this University of Oregon site, visitors can use animated and interactive maps showing various problems, events, developments, and dynamics of American history.

Marsico, Katie. *Andrew Jackson*. New York: Benchmark Books, 2011.
This comprehensive biography conveys facts about Andrew Jackson, and it also relates the history and the culture of the period in which Jackson lived and led.

Morris-Lipsman, Arlene. *Presidential Races: Campaigning for the White House*. Minneapolis: Twenty-First Century Books, 2012.
Morris-Lipsman ushers readers through the most dramatic, influential, and pivotal presidential elections in US history. Political cartoons and photos complement the text.

The Presidents: The White House
http://www.whitehouse.gov/1600/presidents
This official website provides basic biographical information about all the US presidents.

Primary Documents in American History: Library of Congress
http://www.loc.gov/rr/program/bib/ourdocs
Search for original documents relating to Andrew Jackson from the Library of Congress. This site provides links to materials, including images, that relate to topics in this book.

INDEX

PHOTO ACKNOWLEDGMENTS

The images in this book are used with the permission of: Library of Congress, pp. 1 (handwriting), 2 (handwriting), 7, 8, 9, 13, 16, 21, 23, 25, 27, 37, 43 (left), 45, 46, 49, 53, 54, 57, 63, 71, 72, 83, 88, 89; © DEA PICTURE LIBRARY/Getty Images, p. 2 (portrait); © iStockphoto.com/hudiemm (sunburst background); © iStockphoto.com/Nic_Taylor (parchment background); © iStockphoto.com/Phil Cardamone, p. 3 (bunting); © Political Graveyard/flickr.com (CC BY 2.0), p. 3 (signature); Picture History/Newscom, pp. 6, 28; ClipArt ETC, p. 11; © Wikimedia Commons, pp. 17, 85; © Rennett Stowe/flickr.com (CC BY 2.0), p. 18; © North Wind Picture Archives/Alamy, p. 19; © Stock Montage/Getty Images, p. 20; Courtesy Everett Collection, p. 24; Internet Archive Book Images/Wikimedia Commons, p. 30; US Army, p. 31; © Popperfoto/Getty Images, p. 32; Redwood Library & Athenæum, p. 34; © Everett Historical/Shutterstock.com, p. 38; Gift of Thomas Jefferson Coolidge IV in memory of his great-grandfather, Thomas Jefferson Coolidge, his grandfather, Thomas Jefferson Coolidge II, and his father, Thomas Jefferson Coolidge III, courtesy of the Board of Trustees, National Gallery of Art, Washington, DC, p. 40; © Gilder Lehrman Collection, New York, USA/Bridgeman Images, p. 42; © Internet Archive Book Images/flickr.com, p. 43 (right); The Miriam and Ira D. Wallach Division of Art, Prints and Photographs: Print Collection, The New York Public Library, Astor, Lenox and Tilden Foundations, pp. 47, 52, 75; © Heritage Auctions/Wikimedia Commons (CC BY 4.0), p. 50; The Granger Collection, New York, p. 51, 64, 67, 68, 70; © ClassicStock.com/SuperStock, p. 55; Everett Collection/Newscom, p. 58; © AS400 DB/Corbis, p. 59; AISA/Courtesy Everett Collection, p. 78; © Everett Collection Historical/Alamy, p. 80; © The Stapleton Collection/Bridgeman Images, p. 81; © Perry-Castañeda Library, the University of Texas at Austin/Wikimedia Commons, pp. 82; The Hermitage: Home of President Andrew Jackson, Nashville, TN, p. 84; © Cornell University Library/Wikimedia Commons, p. 86; © Joseph Sohm/Shutterstock.com, p. 87.

Front cover: Thomas Sully, Andrew Jackson, Andrew W. Mellon Collection, Image courtesy of the Board of Trustees, National Gallery of Art, Washington, DC, (portrait); © Political Graveyard/flickr.com (CC BY 2.0) (signature); Library of Congress (handwriting); © iStockphoto.com/Phil Cardamone, (flag bunting).

Back cover: © iStockphoto.com/hudiemm (sunburst); © iStockphoto.com/Nic_Taylor (parchment).

ABOUT THE AUTHOR

Christine Zuchora-Walske has been writing and editing books and magazines for children and their parents for twenty–five years. Her author credits include many science books; books exploring the world's nations, US history, and current events; books on pregnancy and parenting; and more. She has also edited hundreds of articles and books in many genres and for all ages. She is especially fond of science and history. But she loves all kinds of knowledge and literature. She never tires of learning new things, and she gets a kick out of trading knowledge with others. Zuchora-Walske lives in Minneapolis, Minnesota, with her husband and two children.